I0489120

Common Sense From A Common Man

The Common Man's Guide to Creating Money

Jacob C. Larson

authorHOUSE®

AuthorHouse™
1663 Liberty Drive
Bloomington, IN 47403
www.authorhouse.com
Phone: 1-800-839-8640

© *2011 Jacob C. Larson. All rights reserved.*

No part of this book may be reproduced, stored in
a retrieval system, or transmitted by any means
without the written permission of the author.

First published by AuthorHouse 3/8/2011

ISBN: 978-1-4567-4425-0 (e)
ISBN: 978-1-4567-4426-7 (sc)

Library of Congress Control Number: 2011903634

Printed in the United States of America

Any people depicted in stock imagery provided by Thinkstock are models,
and such images are being used for illustrative purposes only.
Certain stock imagery © Thinkstock.

This book is printed on acid-free paper.

Because of the dynamic nature of the Internet, any web addresses or
links contained in this book may have changed since publication and
may no longer be valid. The views expressed in this work are solely those
of the author and do not necessarily reflect the views of the publisher,
and the publisher hereby disclaims any responsibility for them.

Dedication:

To David and Nicole –

The road to poverty is riddled with self-doubt, a lack of self-worth, poor decisions, a lack of understanding and fear. Arm yourself with a knowledge of money and how it works. Utilize the tools that God has given you. Become a good steward with what you have created. Share with others what you have learned and most importantly have - No Fear.

Table of Contents

Introduction

What I'm about to say you've probably heard before. But I'm going to say it again. Reading this book and applying its core principals will change your life. I say that in confidence because the principles in this book have been written about and confirmed to work through years of effort brought about through countless people.

These simple, concise principles are often overlooked or devalued. But for those who pay attention, for those who recognize the consistency in what they read or hear, the "secret" of creating money becomes increasingly clear.

This book is about money "creation," *not* merely making money. Anyone can "make" money but by focusing on creating opportunities to increase your cash flow it will ultimately put you in a position to "create" money.

It is with this in mind that I've written this book. After years of "chasing the dollar," this is what I know to be true.

CHAPTER 1

What is Money?

What do you know about money? Have you ever thought about it? I mean, really? Sure, growing up, we hear all sorts of things in regard to it.

As children, we learn quickly that money can get us candy and that we need it to get into the movies. But we also know, based on what we have seen and heard, that the lack of it causes us to worry and stress. Listening to Mom and Dad in the kitchen, we hear all sorts of reasons of why we need it and why it's so important to have it.

Growing up in my house, I learned things a little differently than most kids my age. I was a pastor's kid, a "PK," and the sum total of what I knew about money amounted to: "You can't take it with you," "People are more important" and "God will provide."

In our house, money and material things had very

little value. Don't get me wrong, we were poor, so the need and want of money was present in our home. We just lacked the knowledge to acquire it. And because of our religious beliefs, we chose not to pursue it.

As a kid, those concepts didn't sit well with me. Although I wanted to follow my faith as I was taught, I didn't understand why we had to struggle financially while doing it. I became determined to start working at an early age, odd jobs at first until I could legally be hired. But I was dead set on not living poor. I knew what poverty brought and I didn't want any part of it. I saw first hand what the lack of money brought. And I was at an age where I recognized what having money did.

You may not have grown up as a preacher's kid, but chances are, you've struggled with money, too. Maybe you grew up with fewer resources than your friends. Maybe you've gone from job to job, searching for financial security. Maybe you've always thought that money, and the means of creating it, was mysterious. Maybe you believe that wealthy people keep critical knowledge hidden, just to prevent you from becoming wealthy too.

This book doesn't contain some magic formula. You won't learn how to create money by sitting around and waiting for it to fall from the sky. What you will learn, is how to educate yourself about money, how to work smarter, and how to change your attitude about not only money, but everything in your life.

That's right. Everything. Even your spiritual attitudes or lack of them, will change if you apply the principles in this book. What, you may be asking, does God have to do with money?

Let's go back to where I was as a preacher's kid. The concept of what God would provide didn't sit well with me, because although we always had a roof over our head and food on the table, we lacked. So I questioned our thought processes in regard to money. I questioned the reasoning of our faith. Leaving our ability to live in the hands of the generosity of people who came to our church and paid their tithe once a week in the offering plate seemed less and less like a good idea. I questioned it especially when times were tough for everyone and what came in wasn't enough to cover the basic cost of food for the week.

So after a brief argument with my father, my mother went to apply for government assistance. At the time it was still called welfare. We stood in a long line, seemed like forever at the time, and signed up for food stamps. I didn't know enough to be embarrassed by it. All I knew was that day when we went shopping at the grocery store, it was like Christmas.

We had more food in our fridge than I could remember.

I opened the fridge door and smiled. No more watered-down milk! This was good. This was exciting!

That day came and went however. The reality of our "condition" remained ever present. I learned quickly you can't pay rent or electric bills with food stamps. Then we learned that the government subsidized housing—if your landlord agreed to it. But that required an inspection.

Inspections were great. And I mean that in the most sarcastic way possible.

Let me describe it to you like this so you have a full grasp of what I'm saying. You're a kid in your room, playing with your stuff, being a total angel as I always was, when your mom busts in and starts frantically picking up your toys and clothes and putting them away. Demands that you get up and help her. Her reasoning? We have an inspection. I didn't even know what that was. I just knew it had to be bad.

So my siblings and I would all run around with my mom, trying to straighten the place up. Toys were thrown in closets and closed. Clothes were stuffed under beds and blankets pulled down. Carpets were vacuumed. Then vacuumed again. Don't get me wrong. It wasn't like we lived in a mess; we kids just didn't do much to help my mom out. It seemed as if my mom was *always* cleaning. And with five of us in the house, it was overwhelming for her at times.

So the inspection guy came and did his thing. Filled out his report and left. The only questions I had at the time were, "Did we do good?" "Did we pass?" See, I knew what that meant if we did. I also knew what it meant if we didn't. Our livelihood depended on us passing. And I just wanted to pass. Later when other inspections came we were more prepared and more willing to help Mom manage them. But I'll never forget that first one.

What she had done to provide for our needs was one of the core ideas you'll find in these pages. Where others might be too embarrassed, proud or ashamed to receive assistance, somehow Mom understood the power of giving—and receiving. We'll talk more about that concept in Chapter Four.

In our family, obtaining clothing had its high points too. And we kids were rough on clothes and shoes. Stores like Good Will and the Salvation Army were visited frequently. Not that we never bought "new". But "new to us" seemed to do just fine. Most of the time.

One of my first jobs was working for a carpet cleaning company. I was stoked at the time because technically I was still not quite old enough to get a work permit. But a friend of the family that owned the business was willing to hire me. There was just one minor problem: I needed a uniform.

I was responsible for buying the uniform, which

consisted of a white shirt, easy to obtain, black slacks, also easy to obtain and black shoes. The pair of black shoes was the problem. They *had* to be black. New black shoes cost nearly $50 bucks. At the time it might as well have been $500 bucks. I didn't have it and Mom and Dad didn't either. So Mom, being resourceful and creative as she was, came up with a plan.

I just want to interject; my mom was very cool, very smart when it came to living poor. She knew how to stretch a meal out over three days and could make one pair of pants last for months! She was awesome in that regard.

So when faced with the "shoe" problem, she was the first person I went to. And like I said, she had a plan, so in my mind I was golden, home free. Mom would take care of it. And she did.

We promptly went to Good Will. The problem was, Good Will didn't have any black shoes in stock at the time that fit me. So we moved to plan "B." Plan "B" was simple. We would buy a pair of *not* black shoes for a fraction of the cost of new ones and give them a coat of black shoe polish. Great idea – right? I thought so. And it seemed to work. I showed up on my first day stylin' in my white shirt, black slacks and black shoes. Just like the man had requested. No worries.

Then we did our first job. This was a carpet cleaning

job remember? When cleaning carpet, you're using cleaning products that are designed to remove stains, dirt, soil and oh yeah, *shoe polish*!

Halfway through the job, the guy I was working with noticed my shoes. The black polish around the edge of my shoes had been neatly cleaned off to expose the white soles of my shoes. I was embarrassed. When he asked me about it I knew I needed to come "clean" – no pun intended.

After I explained my predicament, he was very kind and offered to give me an advance on my first paycheck so I could buy some shoes. He gave me the money at the end of my first day and when I got home that's the first thing I did. I bought myself a brand new pair of black shoes. Mom apologized, although it really wasn't her fault. She stepped up and came through to the best of her ability. I never forgot what I learned that day, though.

Maybe you've had times when a necessity arose and the money just wasn't there. You're doing your best to cover all your bases, but now and then the income you stretch and stretch some more, finally snaps. If you don't already do so, this book will show you how you can be more like Mom. She was able to think outside the box. While white shoes dyed with black shoe polish ended up washing away my attempt to dress according to the job's code, my boss clearly saw that I'd tried my very best.

I didn't whine that I couldn't afford black shoes, or

just wear the white-soled pair and hope no one noticed. My boss understood that I was willing (with Mom's help) to go beyond the obvious. To think outside the box. We'll talk more about this in Chapter Five.

Transportation was always an adventure in my house too. The strange thing about vehicles is they require maintenance. And they don't seem to care when or how they get it. When they need it they seem content to just let the world pass by until they get it. As a result, I learned to be somewhat of a mechanic. From pulling and replacing starters, testing and replacing batteries, brakes, carburetors, pulling and replacing spark plugs to full blown let's pull the engine and rebuild it.

Problem was I hated mechanic work. Never liked doing it when it needed to be done or the filthy hands and busted knuckles it gave you when doing it. So even though I learned how to do a lot of it I always played dumb when someone needed something done to a vehicle so they wouldn't ask the strapping young man (their words) I was to do it. Because doing it for the other people we knew consisted of being paid with a "thank you" and "you have such a great boy."

Neither of which I had much use for at the time. My dad, however, knew I was capable and he wouldn't hesitate to muck up a Saturday with an all-day project on the car that he would assure me before we'd start would only take a couple of hours.

We did have some good times though. In between the busted knuckles and brief rants when things didn't go right. I learned the value of – keeping *everything*: every nut, every screw, every wire, every hose no matter how big or how small even if you didn't know what it could be used for, you never knew when you were going to need it. As a result, my dad had boxes of old parts and hoses and stuff. I also learned that black electrical tape *fixes* everything! Did you bust your knuckles or cut your finger? No worries, wrap that sucker in electrical tape – problem solved. And we didn't own an extension cord that didn't have some of it on it. When I was a kid I just thought they were sold that way. Black electrical tape and WD-40 were the two main items that my dad always carried in his tool box. If you had those, you were set for the road!

So why am I telling you all this? Because you know what I've learned about money? I've learned that regardless of what you may hear some people say about it, money dictates what clothes you wear, what food you eat, where you live, what cars you drive. And if you look at it closer, money is what provides the roads you drive on, the schools you go to, the churches you attend, and so on. Money.

The lack or excess of it provides all those things listed above and more.

Money is a "tool" that is used to obtain the goods and services you need, want and desire to live your life the way you choose to live it. Money is *not* evil. And those that regard it as such are fools who either don't understand its positive use or are unwilling to take the steps needed to acquire it.

Money offers an exchange among honorable people for goods and services rendered. Money will boost a person's confidence and self esteem when acquired properly and the lack of it will rob a person of their well being and destroy their very soul when obtained through unfavorable means.

Money does not discriminate between people or races; nor does it provide what it is incapable of providing. It is the driving force behind every thing that is "good" and every thing that is "evil." It is the "tool" that people use to make all those things possible. It knows its place in this world.

Because of that, it's important that *you* take it seriously. Because of that, it is important for you to know and learn of its proper use. Because of that, money *should be* the number one topic studied in school. Because of that, it *should be* regarded as an ally, as a friend. And if you're honest enough with yourself to recognize that, then your thoughts about money may need to change and your education of it should begin.

The lack or excess of money will always be a part of your life. And maybe like me, you have some "issues" with it that you may need to come to terms with. Regardless of what you need to reckon with, it's up to you to study it.

It's up to you to learn how to manage it. It can't and won't be done for you.

You can attempt to ignore it or speak out against it but it won't change much for you until you truly recognize its value. You must *choose* to utilize it the way it is intended to be regarded and used – as a "tool". It's your choice.

So where do you start? Read.

CHAPTER 2

Develop a reading habit

I was never much of a reader growing up. I mean, sure, for school, but outside of that? Nada. I always seemed to be able to find more interesting things to do with my time and I figured guys my age that read either didn't have a TV or hadn't discovered girls. At any rate, I didn't do it – ever.

But while working in various jobs, I was smart enough to ask questions, one of which was, "How did you get to where you are"?

Seemed like a simple question at the time. I got all sorts of answers.

Most of these answers entailed working hard, getting a good job and waiting years to get promoted. Only then, these people assured me, would the money come.

But the reality was, I didn't want to wait. Working

hard didn't worry me. Getting a good job seemed simple enough. But the waiting part of the answer always kind of miffed me. I didn't want to simply wait for time to run its course. The thought repulsed me. The concept of time slipping away was already deep-seated in me.

A preacher's kid never knows when it's the end of the world, you know? Besides, I still had plenty of stuff I wanted to do before Jesus came back.

So I asked this guy my question, a guy that at the time I regarded as "rich." He looked at me and said, "You really want to know?"

I blurted out an enthusiastic, "Yes!" I thought he was really going to tell me the "secret" to his success. I thought he was going to share how he actually made his money.

He looked at me and said, "Read."

My heart sank. I was dumbfounded. I repeated what he said as if to question what I had heard. He repeated his answer, followed with a yes.

I said, "Read what?"

He reached into his briefcase and pulled out a book. And he said, "You can start by reading this."

I just looked at the book and then explained to him in great detail how I did *not* read books. I told him reading was boring and pointless and that I thought it was a complete waste of time, effort and energy.

Reading was something I was required to do in school.

Since I was no longer a student, the concept of reading for actually learning something eluded me. I respectfully declined his generous offer.

A couple of days later, still chapped by the conversation, I told him, "Hey, look I'm not interested in reading a bunch of books, I just want to know how you became rich. Why won't you just tell me?"

He said that he already had told me. "Read."

I was getting flustered. "But I hate reading books."

He looked at me and said, "I didn't ask you if you *liked* to read. You wanted to know how I became rich. I offered you a way for you to do that."

I'll never forget what he said next. "If you're unwilling to do the things that rich people do, you'll never become one!"

"*If you're unwilling to do the things that rich people do, you'll never become one.*"

Now *that* caught my attention. So, I repeated back what I thought he'd said. "So, you're saying if I read this book I'll be rich?"

And he said, "This book, and many others—yes. You need to develop a reading *habit*. You don't have to like it but you do have to read. Rich people read. You want to become rich—read."

I took the book called, *The Choice* by Og Mandino. It was the first book I had ever read after graduating high school. This book changed my life. I developed a reading habit.

I don't necessarily care for every book that I've read but I always finish them. It's a discipline that I have worked at and believe to have mastered. I often read multiple books at the same time. Over the years I have read more books than I can remember. My speed has gotten faster and my comprehension is much better. It has been by far the most valuable piece of information in regard to the acquiring of money that I have learned. Reading is such a simple thing. But I had overlooked it as a way to put myself in a better position to generate the money I wanted.

So what are you reading? Maybe like me, you don't like to read. Who cares? Read. Just do it. Don't make excuses or try to ignore it. Get it done! You don't have to like it. "Like" has nothing to do with it. If you don't like how you're living, how you're eating, what car you're driving, you had better start learning about different ways of doing things or you're going to be going around the same mountain, over and over. It's that simple.

The subject matter you look for in a book isn't that important at first. Sure, you should be reading stuff that pertains to making and managing money.

After all, this book you have in your hands is about money. But the point is to develop a reading habit! And that means you may have to mix it up a bit so you stay focused on what you're trying to accomplish. Believe it or not, even a classic novel like *Atlas Shrugged*, by Ayn Rand, while long, can help you understand the financial world and your part in it.

Start out slow, read something, ten or fifteen minutes a day, then add to it. And don't even try and use time as an excuse! You know what? Everyone has the same twenty-four hours each day. Most people find the time to do what they want to do. If you're serious about learning to create money, you'll find the time.

Work to develop a reading habit so that it becomes something you want to do. If nothing else, instead of gabbing with your co-workers on your lunch break, *choose* to read. If you want to get some strange looks, start holing up on your breaks with a book. In a few days, they'll go back to gabbing while you start making progress.

However you implement a reading habit, don't spend

one more minute of one more hour of one more day, wondering, waiting for something to happen or change in your life that will somehow change the course of your financial picture. It's up to you to act.

Don't sit and wait for it to happen. Read. It will change your outlook. It will give you the information necessary to properly utilize money as a "tool." It will change your current financial circumstances. It will give you hope and make your financial future look bright. I guarantee you.

Test it. Then write me and tell me of your response. You can contact me through my website: www. buycommonsense.com . I want to know.

What you don't want to do is pick up one book, read it and stop there! Remember, the information your seeking in regards to creating money can't be found in one book. Different books take on different angles or aspects of it. Different authors explain different topics and different readers pick up on different things. So, don't cut yourself short. You may not be in a brick and mortar school building or classroom but you have homework to do and you're still a student. So learn it, study the material. When you're done, seek out more reading material.

In time, if you're anything like me, you'll begin to see a pattern in everything you read in relation to money. The basics will remain the same and have done so for hundreds of years.

You're simply a new student of them and "money laws" learned without the benefit of a formal education (meaning through a book) are hard learned. I'd rather you encounter the solution to a financial problem through a page in a book than on the cold, hard streets of life. And *that* is what you'll be left with—if you don't read.

Developing a reading habit should be your number one priority, starting with this book. The second thing you need to do is recommend this book to your friends and family so they'll read it too. No, I'm not trying to be coy.

This isn't the only book you're going to read, right? We've established that. You're going to be reading a lot of books right? And I'm assuming you have friends and family that will benefit from what you're going to be learning. And you do care about them, don't you?

Then encourage them to utilize the tools they have like you're doing. Encourage them to read. Share your books with them so they too can read the information you're learning. Before you know it, you'll be opening up doors to all sorts of conversations with them, conversations that can jump-start creation and development of money. These ideas will push you, drive you toward a common goal, a common purpose, resulting in new and exciting ways to create money. Reading and then sharing this reading habit with those around you is part of a journey that can change the financial picture of everyone involved.

Here's a partial reading list to help you get started: Remember, there are books, magazines, newspapers and internet postings available on every aspect of financial health. Be a seeker and don't settle for only reading what's placed in front of you.

Carnegie, Dale, *How to Win Friends and Influence People*, Reissue Edition, New York, Simon & Schuster, 2009.

Clason, George S., *The Richest Man in Babylon*, New York, Signet Books, 2004.

Gerber, Michael E., *The E Myth Revisited*, Harper Collins, Third Edition,1995.

Hill, Napoleon, *Think and Grow Rich*, Rev Exp, New York, Tarcher, 2005.

Kiyosaki, Robert, *Rich Dad, Poor Dad*, Business Plus, 2010.

Kyne, Peter, *The Go Getter*, ReadaClassic.com, 2010, orig. 1921 published by Wm. Randolph Hearst.

Littauer, Florence, *Your Personality Tree*, Thomas Nelson Publishers, Nashville, 1989.

Mandino, Og, *The Choice*, New York, Bantam Books, 1986.

Mandino, Og, *The Greatest Salesman in the World*, New York, Bantam Books, 1974.

Peter, Laurence J. Peter, *The Peter Principle*, New York, Harper Business, 2009.

Stanley, Thomas, *The Millionaire Next Door,* Taylor Trade Publishing, 2010, Reissue.

Tyson, Eric, *Personal Finance for Dummies*, New York, For Dummies, 2009.

CHAPTER 3

Mind your Association

Remember that kid in school who your momma always warned you about? Most people refer to him as "Little Johnny." Yeah, remember him? The wild kid that was always getting into trouble? Your momma would tell you to stay away from that kid, that by hanging out with him you'd just get in trouble, right?

Well guess what? You may be considered an adult now but Little Johnny is grown up too. And he's still all the trouble and more that your momma said he'd be. Problem is, his real name isn't "Johnny" His real name generally is different and is followed up by descriptive words bearing a title such as: my friend, my co-worker, my aunt, my uncle, my niece, my mom, my dad, my sister, my brother, my spouse, etc. You getting the idea here?

Sometimes the people you have in your life may be

the absolute *best* when it comes to having fun, relaxing or doing a specific task. Yet when it comes to finances they can be the worst possible people for you to associate with or take advice from. Does that make sense?

Let me explain it this way: Let's say you want to learn how to play football. What you're hoping to learn is how to properly throw a spiral ball. Are you going to ask your grandma (who's never touched a football in her life) to teach you?

Or are you going to seek out the advice from a quarterback? If you want to learn to fly a plane, are you going to ask your friend or co-worker (who's never ridden on a plane, let alone flown one) how to fly one or are you going to ask a pilot? You see where I'm going with this?

One of the cool things about friends and family and co-workers, is they're *always* willing to talk with you and give you advice. There is only problem.

Advice from people you know is not always *sound* advice. When it comes to finances, if they are as "cash" poor as you are, it's *never* sound advice. Why would you take advice or listen to people without money when you're trying to acquire a means in which to create money?

Don't get me wrong. I'm not saying the people you choose to hang out with are bad people, but when it comes to creating money, unless they have it and know how to acquire it, their advice isn't going to be useful. Don't listen to it.

Now why would I say that? Because some of the most challenging times in my life stemmed from my association with poor and "broke" people. Some people are poor only in one area—that of cash. When I say poor people what I mean is they're "cash poor." They may be rich in talent, in intelligence, ideas, enthusiasm or other ways. But as far as money goes, they're poor. Do you know what I mean?

Cash poor people may not have the finances but mentally they are still optimistic about their ability to create money. For them, the glass is always half-full. They haven't given up, or decided nothing will ever change. Cash poor people are still working hard to generate cash flow, although you may not be able to see their efforts producing just yet.

On the other hand, people I classify as mentally broke are literally hopeless for the future, the glass half-empty folks. They're incapable of seeing anything other than their current situation. They have nothing to offer you other than negativity about a situation. They will always give you reasons why something won't work. They'll always offer excuses as to why they're in a situation and they seldom see things getting better. Things only get worse with them. Stay away from them.

That's right! Stay absolutely, positively away from them to the best of your ability. That doesn't mean your going to stop loving or caring about Uncle Johnny. That doesn't mean at family get-togethers you're not going to talk to Uncle Johnny. That doesn't mean you're going to call Uncle Johnny up and say, "Hey, love you and all but you're financially broke, so I'm not going to associate with you because I don't want you bringing me down!"

No. It simply means that you going to assess the people in your life from a financial perspective. If they fall into the "mentally broke" category, you're going to recognize it and not discuss finances with them. Get it?

Uncle Johnny may be the best fisherman on the planet. Great. When you're around him, talk fishing. But if he isn't living the life you want to live *financially,* don't get sucked into his life. Don't sit around and complain or grumble about how bad his job or the economy is. Don't do it. Do you understand the difference?

Remember, if your already cash poor, what benefit are you going to get from talking to someone that's in the same situation that you are? Learning this is critical. Because when you start to recognize the people in your life from a financial perspective you'll realize two things. Number one, you'll recognize who you may care about but shouldn't associate too much with. So you'll distance your self from them.

Number two, you'll recognize your need for positive reinforcement and you'll seek out people who aren't mentally "broke" to be a part of your association. You'll seek out people that are on the same wave length as you, determined and focused, working toward a common goal, a common purpose and they will become a part of your own personal "counsel."

Your "Counsel." I've said it to various people over the course of various topics for a number of years. It is something I picked up during the course of my reading and studying and is a truth that has always stuck with me. And that is this: Never counsel with your own thoughts. YOU are your own worst critic.

In your quest for creating money, you're going to come across challenges that will stretch your mind, knowledge, and your comfort level. If you choose to rely on yourself and what you know, chances are you're going to make mistakes. Not only that, your recovery is going to take longer.

Why? Put simply, because you're in the midst of it. You're too heavily engaged in the situation to get an accurate view of what is going on. Because of that, how to remedy or enhance it may not be clear to you. Set your ego aside and seek "counsel."

Think about it. *Everyone* in a place of wealth has counsel—*everyone*. Some times that "counsel" is called a board of directors or a mentor or a financial advisor. But make no mistake. Everyone in a place of wealth has a counsel.

And they utilize that counsel whenever the need arises.

Never counsel with your own thoughts. YOU are your own worst critic.

So, who is your "counsel?" Who is a part of that small group of people in regard to finances who share the same common goal, the same common purpose as you? Who has the lifestyle you want? Who is your go-to person, the one you're able to pull sound advice from? Who? If you can't answer that question directly and in short order, chances are you don't have one.

What are you waiting for? Still waiting on Grandma to learn how to throw a spiral? Or are you going to seek out a quarterback? You don't have to wait to be financially successful before you establish your counsel.

Trust me—your counsel will change over time. It will expand and contract. You will have some that you will include at the present moment, then after some assessment, you'll remove and replace them. That's normal and it's a good thing. It means your staying "tuned" into the wellness of your counsel members. But you must have them.

They will be your greatest asset. They will not only help propel you to a place of financial peace that you're seeking but they will also help you avoid common financial pitfalls.

Establishing and maintaining a solid counsel is key to creating money.

So who do you talk to in order to establish your counsel? What do you say to that prospective counsel? If you think about it, the answers to these questions are easy. Remember, you're looking for someone who currently has what you want financially. So the people you want to talk to need to be somewhat established. Determining who that is generally is pretty easy.

You may already have come in contact with some of them. Chances are you have. The hard part is going to be finding a way to get them to talk to you. Remember, these people are already successful at some level. They already have something you want, already have an established and maintained counsel of their own. In short—they don't need you, you need them. Your understanding of that will help you in your approach.

So how do you go about finding a trusted counsel?

I've found that a great way of opening the dialogue with someone I want and need to talk to is to offer to take them to lunch. I offer, making sure we both understand that even though they may be worth millions, I'm buying them lunch. Again, they don't need me, I need them. So, they eat on me.

Second, if they agree to meet, then the time and location is up to them. By making the lunch convenient for them, I'm sending the message that I'm serious. I will drive anywhere, at any time, day or night to get what I want. The burden of what may be an inconvenience should be on me, not the person whose time I'm requesting.

The other part of the equation is this: Don't try to establish someone as a part of your counsel by asking them for money or trying to get them to invest in what you're doing. This is not to say that after talking with you and getting to know you they may be interested in doing that. But your purpose in meeting with them is to establish them as a source of sound information. You want what they *know*, what's in their head, not their money.

Unless you know how to acquire or manage it, they could give you money and it would be wasted. The person you're meeting with knows this. Don't embarrass yourself by making your contact tell you this fact. You're meeting with them to get them to tell you what they *know*, how they got *started* and what their *plans* are.

So ask them those questions. Then shut up and listen. Take notes. Listen to them tell you their story and use what you can. It may not all apply but you can glean from every conversation various truths that will help you in your journey. The point is once you have a meeting like this set up, make sure you're undistracted and present.

If a lunch meeting doesn't work, try something else. Just find a way to open that line of communication with someone in a position to act as your counsel. At the time I don't necessarily explain to them that is what I'm doing. I do make it very clear that I want to know what they know and I make it a point to exchange contact information.

That way, later when I need some advice, they're only a phone call or email away and they remember me.

Once you establish a counsel you'll discover something. You'll discover that your counsel has a counsel! They currently have people that they work with on a routine basis. And if you establish yourself correctly and prove yourself a worthy business associate, they will refer you to members of their counsel.

This is huge when it happens, so don't muck it up! Treat the people you're referred to with just as much respect as you did your initial contact. Doing this will broaden your list of people who will be in your corner when the need arises.

If you came into a million dollars tomorrow, who would you call? Do you even know what to do with that much money—besides spend it? How could you take that million and turn it into two million? Do you have any idea?

Establish a counsel and you will. Establish a counsel and you will know exactly who to call to help you and why you're calling them. Over time you will become a part of someone's counsel. And the information you have gleaned over years of your positive association with your own counsel will assist you in being considered good counsel.

That isn't to say that you're going to do everything

your counsel suggests or tells you to do. Or that when you're counsel for someone else, that they will always listen to or take your advice. That's not always true. One thing about establishing a counsel is they tend to know their place. You're going to do what you're going to do and you'll have the consequences your actions bring. Their job is to offer what they know.

Your job is to take what they know, dissect it and use it to fulfill your purpose, whatever that may be. And in doing that you'll discover exactly what that purpose truly is.

CHAPTER 4

The Power of Giving

One thing that has remained consistent in everything I have read has been the concept of giving. Like most people, at first, my response to it was always the same. Giving? Sure, after I make some money, I'll be happy to give back. The problem with that rationale, that I only discovered later, was that it was backwards.

Don't get me wrong, I'm not suggesting that you give in order to get. Not at all. But what I am saying is that in reading about different successful people who always seemed to be so big on giving I missed the key element in the process that they were describing. The underlying trait in everything they say in regard to giving stems from their belief in another unseen, unwritten law that is immediately set into motion when someone chooses to give. It's the law of receiving.

The law of receiving. This is something that I struggled to understand.

See, I knew how to give. Giving or the concept of giving had been deeply engrained in me as a child. The part of giving that I had a hard time with doing was receiving.

Let me explain. When I was growing up as a preacher's kid, encountering people in need was a common occurrence. As I was taught, I always did what I could via money or service in the needed help of others.

What I didn't do well was receive.

Receiving giving, for me, was very difficult. My pride prevented me from accepting offers from others and because of that, declining those offers became a habit. My default response to someone offering to give to me was, "Thanks but I'll be fine." I also found myself actually volunteering to take on the burden. When going out to lunch or dinner with friends I would automatically reach for the bill! Even if they invited me, I would feel the need to pay.

See, for me, paying the bill was a lot easier than receiving the gesture of someone paying it for me. As a result, I grew accustom to picking up the tab regardless of what I was doing or who I was meeting with.

The summer of 2006, I met a guy who changed my thought process on the subject of giving. His name was

Fred. Fred was a very tall guy, well over six feet tall. His presence was intimidating. Besides being tall, he was an ex-cop so his personal demeanor exuded confidence. I met him at a garage sale. We started talking, very cordially at first, about random stuff, nothing special. Then he said something that caught my attention.

He said he had six Saturdays and one Sunday every week. I knew exactly what he meant when he said it and I promptly requested a meeting. We set up a time and place to meet during a work day when his favorite soup, clam chowder, was on the menu.

During our first meeting I probed him for what he did to get six Saturdays and one Sunday. He recommended some books for me to read. Some that he mentioned I had previously read. He told me to read them again. I did. I continued to meet him every Thursday for breakfast once each week for nearly six months. The only meal I had bought him was that first one. After that, he insisted on paying.

This was difficult at first for me. Fred and I went round and round about it for weeks. When I finally conceded that he would be paying, I stopped asking.

We talked about a variety of stuff during that time. On more than one occasion he called me a very wise young man. After a bit, the concept of me being "wise" didn't really set well with me, nor did his incessant insistence of paying. When I asked him about it, he seemed to talk in circles.

So, I jammed him about it, and that's putting it mildly. I didn't understand why he was willing to meet with me every week, or why he said some of the things he'd say about me. I confronted him with such fervor that at one point he flinched, thinking I was coming across the table at him. Finally when I stopped talking he looked at me, smiled and said, "You done?"

I sat back in my chair and mustered up a, "Yeah."

He said, "Jacob, you're a giver, that much is true but you don't know how to receive. Because of that, all the giving you're doing is wasted. Just like money that is given to people who don't know what to do with it; your giving bears no fruit because when it comes back to you, you kill it."

I sat there, stunned.

He continued. "I've been taking time out of my day; buying you breakfast, every week for weeks and you've done nothing but fight me tooth and nail every time we meet." When he said this, I got a little defensive and told him he didn't have to, that I would have gladly paid for the meals. He said I was missing the point. He said, "I've met with you and bought your meals to teach you how to receive."

That was the last meeting I had with the man.

And for a long time his words haunted me. I spent days and nights trying to grasp what he was saying. Just trying to wrap my brain around it. Finally, the tall man's words began to make sense to me. And that's what I want you to know.

What I've found is that "giving" is about "receiving" too.

People who are willing to give are in a sense telling you that you are worthy of receipt. By their very act of willingness to give to you they are saying in confidence that their "seed" will not be wasted. That you are a worthy person to give to because you know how to receive and that in your receiving you will in turn *give.*

When engaging in the act of giving you unconsciously set in motion a chain of events that takes place in what is unseen. This is a hard thing to describe and many authors choose their words carefully when trying to describe it.

But based on what I've read, it doesn't matter as much how you describe it as how you apply it. Call it Karma, Infinite Intelligence, The Cosmos, God, The Force, Divine Intelligence, Higher Power—the list goes on. The act of giving sends out seeds into God or the Divine or whatever term you use to describe something outside yourself. These seeds result in receiving.

This is the unseen, unwritten law of giving and

receiving: when you give, you will receive. The thing is, you have to learn to receive or your giving is wasted.

In the same manner that money given to people untrained in its proper use is wasted, receiving given to people untrained in giving is wasted. The two go hand in hand.

For me, receiving was the problem. It was the one part of the equation I was unaccustomed to. For others it is the giving part that they struggle with. Both parts of the equation are required for the law of giving and receiving to work properly. Recognizing this is key to tapping into that unseen power that manages it all.

This is the unseen, unwritten law of giving and receiving: when you give, you will receive. The thing is, you have to learn to receive or your giving is wasted.

When you give, give expecting nothing in return. If you give expressly to get something back, it's nice that you gave, but the law doesn't work that way. When you give freely, with *no strings attached*, you will get a return. This return may not come from the place you expected or in the time frame you specify. In fact, the return may be something altogether different than you imagined. But it will return. Receive with appreciation and the understanding that you are receiving because you know how to give.

As a result, you will find yourself in a position of receiving with the ability to give more! That's just how it works. And there is no greater purpose of creating money - than giving.

In fact, when you think about it, if you really care about the sick, the poor, the homeless, your task of creating money – is a must. Instead of working to give just 10%, work to create money so that you can give 90% and live on 10%. After the home, the boat, the car, the vacation is all bought and paid for – what else is there?

With that in mind, giving should be something you start doing right now.

Maybe now financially you can't – no worries. Donate your time. Offer what you can but make it a part of what you do. Open the door to the laws of giving and receiving. You start by giving. In time, opportunities to receive will come to you. Some opportunities will come in the form of money, some in the form of a meeting, or an interview, or an invitation. Whatever the form, be willing to receive. When those opportunities come, be willing to say, "Yes!"

Also, say, "Thank You!" Show your appreciation. But don't sell your self short. Remember, if the opportunity to receive has come to you, it's because you have proven yourself worthy of receipt. Receive it and use that opportunity to increase your ability to give.

There is no greater reason to create money.

Chapter 5

Think Outside the "Box"

People who are truly successful rarely follow the crowd. They always seem to follow the beat of their own drum. Sure, they may follow a specific system or format, but they apply that system in their own unique way. They learn and practice thinking outside of the box but they don't limit this way of thinking to only their business dealings. Successful people generally apply this "thinking outside the box" principle to everything that they do. So in order for you to mirror or surpass their results, you need to learn to think the same way.

As I've mentioned, I've attended various business seminars and listened to various speakers teach about creating money. I'd sometimes leave these gatherings with the feeling that I wasn't being told the whole story. This was somewhat frustrating to me as some of those functions had cost me my time and my hard-earned money. I was determined to find out about this missing piece of the puzzle.

In every seminar or lecture about creating money, the part that always seemed to be left out was the specific "thing" that a person needed to *do* to create money. In my mind, I was waiting to hear about a certain job, career or business that was the secret to creating money.

In these groups, the speaker never identified the one "secret" I thought I needed to hear. I believed that all I needed was the "right" information. I'd know exactly what to do to become successful, if only I could unlock this secret.

What I've discovered, after multiple guesses and tries is – there isn't one.

There isn't just *one thing* that you can do that will slingshot you into creating money – there are *tons*! Why? Because successful people, applying success principles into anything they try, will become successful!

The secret of creating money is an attitude; a presence, a discipline. Successful people adopt and learn specific character traits, that when applied to any task they take on, produces results.

By adopting the same principles successful people employ, you can begin to develop an attitude, discipline and presence in your efforts to create money. Like me, you'll probably go through some trial and error as you reinvent yourself with regard to creating money. Along the way you'll discover as I did, that some methods do work better at creating money than others!

Let me explain. Nearly fifteen years ago, I was working for a local motor coach manufacturer. I had been hired to install "felt" into the inside of the cargo bays of the lower part of the coaches.

At the company's request, I received a week of instruction, although I had a pretty good handle on things by the end of my first day. After my week of training was completed I was on my own and that's when the fun started. See, working for a motor coach manufacturer was not my life-long dream but I needed the money so I took the job.

Once I was hired though, I knew I needed to free up some time to explore other options and after my week of training was done that's just what I started to do.

I began by watching the assembly line. I noted how fast it moved, when it moved and how many coaches my area was required to do on a daily basis to keep the line moving and not bring attention to myself. My goal wasn't to figure out ways to goof off on company time. I just needed to be able to do my job well and still carve out enough time to consider my future.

The first thing I discovered was that in short order I

could measure, cut and install the felt into two and a half coaches a day. This benchmark of two and a half coaches per day was what was expected and required of my job to keep the line moving to each area efficiently.

Problem was, I didn't want to spend my entire day measuring, cutting and installing felt. I needed to cut my time and I knew it. So I started taking a record of each coach type and took note of their variation. I realized that there were three main coach types and each type had bay measurements that were similar to each other. With each specific coach type I made notes and listed the number of cargo bays it had and what the measurements for it were.

Then I acquired some cardboard and made templates. This meant – no more time wasted measuring. At the beginning of each day I would do a quick walk of the line, see what style of coach was coming through the line that day and promptly cut out enough felt for two days worth of coaches.

As the coach would roll into my area I would sweep out each bay, spray the glue and fit in my precut felt. And guess what? In one week of having the job turned over to me – I could finish my job before noon.

I had my "time." Now I had to just figure out how to use it. I was already spending my lunch break alone. I rarely ate in the cafeteria with the other employees. I was labeled anti-social. I would generally sneak unnoticed into one of the coaches and spend my thirty minute lunchtime reading.

But a thirty minute lunch break goes by quickly, especially when you're in the middle of a good book! I needed a place to go where I would be uninterrupted. After some thought, I came up with a solution.

Remember my templates that I made out of card board? I discovered that when covered in felt, placed in a bay with the edges tucked in – they looked like a wall. Behind this "wall" was plenty of room to lay back and read. I promptly made fake walls to fit into the cargo bays for each style of coach on my line.

Each day I finished my job by noon and then retired to a cargo bay and put up my fake wall. It worked! The coach manufacturer was getting its much needed job done and done well, and I was getting my time to read. I couldn't tell you how many times, while reading a book, that I was interrupted by someone actually working in the cargo bay I was in! No one spotted me or questioned the wall. Everyone must have thought the variation in the depth of the cargo bay for that specific coach was a special order! I worked there for two years. To this day, no one has ever said that they knew I was behind that fake wall, reading.

Your job may be a lot different than mine was. Maybe

you're saying you could never disappear during your shift in order to read a book. But that's not the point.

The real point is that it doesn't matter what you do for a job. Whether it's a job, a career (another term for a job), a business, whatever, you need to understand them for what they are: vehicles.

They are means with which you generate money. They are "vehicles."

Vehicles get you where you want to go. Because of this, you should not only drive your vehicle to the best of your ability, you shouldn't care about what that vehicle is or how it looks as long as it makes you money.

That's *all* a job is – a money-making vehicle. True, some vehicles run better than others. The reality is that jobs which tend to run hard and strong to cash are often overlooked. They're overlooked because of things like pride and personal self-worth.

Pride and personal self-worth are two things that are very expensive to obtain and manage when derived from what you *do*. Neither of these qualities is accurate when used in the context of a vehicle which describes you. Who you are and what you are does not come from what you do! People who derive their personal self-worth from the vehicle they have chosen to drive are ignorant.

So let's look at some different "vehicles," shall we?

The most common vehicle driven by the majority of

the population is that of a job. Jobs are the easiest vehicles to get and drive. You fill out an application, show up, do your job and get a paycheck. Not necessarily a bad thing as a way to make money but for "creating" money they leave much to be desired.

Why? Each job you get, regardless of the pay, comes with an invisible ceiling. That ceiling consists of twenty-four hours in a day, seven days a week and 365 days a year. If you could work all those hours: twenty-four each day, seven days a week, 365 days a year, you could multiply your hourly pay rate by the maximum possible work hours. The total represents the most you could ever make while doing that job. Does that number excite you?

Sure, the number is probably *way* more than what you're used to making. But right away you know this number is also highly unlikely—you're not Superman or Wonder Woman. You can't work 24 hrs a day, 7 days a week, 365 days a year, unless you're a mom or a nanny. The reality is that you'll probably work from 40-60 hours per week. This means you're actually going to be making much less than the maximum.

The "raises" you may get from a job for good performance generally don't even keep up with inflation, do they? At most companies, these now-and-then raises are cancelled by various pay cuts which probably occur more often than a pay raise.

How about these examples? Your paycheck is cut with every rate increase of your personal or group insurance. Every tax increase imposed on you is a pay cut. Every percentage of increased interest you pay is a pay cut. With pay cuts everywhere you turn, in a sense the more time you spend at that job the more money you are losing.

So how is a job as a vehicle for creating money? Not very good is it? A job is a temporary fix – to a permanent problem.

You *can* use a job to slow down a financial leak and you can use it to your advantage. That's what I did when I worked for the motor coach manufacturer. But in order to use a job as a stepping stone to success, you need to focus on your ultimate goal and think outside of the box!

Maybe right now you have to work a nine-to-five job, or a job with not much of a future. Don't worry! Recognize the job for what it is and use it to your advantage. Let the job be the vehicle that helps you get where you want to go. Eventually though, your goal should be to get out. Your goal should be to step away from the vehicle, as soon as possible!

In working a job you could say you're allowing yourself to be a passenger of the vehicle.

You don't really have control of which direction or fast that vehicle is going. To create money you need to become the *driver*. Self-employment offers you that control.

Self-employment puts you in the vehicle's driver's seat. Driving the vehicle will bring you much closer, much faster to your goal of creating money through the marketing and sales of your specific goods or service. But how does it do that? By putting you in a position to increase the revenue you generate through an increase of time. Let me explain: Which would you prefer? One hundred percent of your own effort? Or one percent of one hundred people's effort?

> *Successful people think outside the box. Being self-employed gives these people the necessary time and flexibility they need for this kind of thought.*

When working a regular job, you are in a sense using one hundred percent of your own time and effort to earn revenue (expendable cash). When you become self-employed you're in a sense, leveraging, other people's time and effort to increase your ability to *create* revenue. I say create revenue as opposed to earn revenue because successful self-employment requires creative thought. It demands thinking outside of the box!

In fact, more than ninety percent of all millionaires are self-employed! Ninety percent! That's huge! That should give you a clue as to how successful people think—and it's a huge tip in regard to creating money. Successful people think outside the box. Being self-employed gives these people the necessary time and flexibility they need for this kind of thought.

In your quest for creating money, your need or desire to be self-employed should be right at the top of the list. You should be focused and working toward that goal every day.

How can you work toward self-employment? First, be willing to do what other people are unwilling to do. Remember, if the "masses" are doing it, chances are it doesn't fall into the category of what that other ten percent are doing that made them millionaires. Actively seek self-employment by thinking outside of the box.

To simplify things a bit I'll break down self-employment into two categories – providing a "service" or producing a "good." When you start out, look at the skills and resources (meaning cash) you have available. If your expendable resources are limited you may need to start by providing a "service," preferably one that is consistent or follows along the lines of a specific skill that you have acquired. In a sense, you're creating a job for yourself, with you as the owner and the employee. But won't that cause you to work too hard and too long?

Absolutely not! Don't worry—with you now in the driver's seat of your own self-employment vehicle, you can now leverage other people's time. With every addition of a new employee you gain more expendable time. This is time to get something done, to increase your ability to generate more revenue through that employee's production.

So, if you have eight expendable hours in your day and you hire someone to work for you leveraging eight expendable hours of their day, you now have sixteen total available expendable hours at your disposal! It's definitely a great start towards creating money. But this start also has its disadvantages too.

With every new employee whose time and production you leverage you are also increasing your liability and even though you have increased *your* overall time, you're still bound by that invisible "box" that managing time inevitably brings, which is why when considering self-employment, providing a service is the less favorable of the two.

Producing a "good" is by far the most favorable means of self-employment.

By marketing and selling a "good" you are breaking the barriers of geography and transcending time. The metaphorical "box" we have been discussing in regards to time - no longer exists.

Music, movies, books, food, vehicles, cell phones, toilet paper, or you-name-it: these are all merchandise or *goods* being marketed and sold to the masses. Millions of people all over the world contribute a percentage of every dollar spent towards the purchase of goods every day. and guess where that percentage goes to? That's right – the person selling that merchandise. Is there more to it? Sure! There is a lot more, but that is the basics of it. Your focus should be toward the goal of self-employment that markets goods.

The biggest challenge when it comes to this area of self-employment is cash. To effectively produce and market a good requires expendable cash. If you currently have expendable resources available to you, then self-employment may be easier for you to step into.

Most people do not have expendable resources at first. For this reason, the majority of small business owners get their start in self-employment by providing a service. On the surface it may seem as if you're forced to begin self-employment with the less-desirable option.

Don't let this prevent you from becoming self-employed. Remember, even if providing a service is all that is available to you right now, you'll still be moving in the right direction toward creating money. You will have increased your expendable time, which frees you to at some point take the next step.

Eventually, using the time and resources that you have created in providing your service, you will be able to tap into the area of self-employment that allows you to market and sell a good.

The point is that while doing whatever you've chosen to do, you do it with your mind focused on the long term results of what you're trying to accomplish. Constantly look for ways and means to assist you in your journey of creating money. Utilize every opportunity toward assisting you in your goal. Think outside the box. Don't get hung up or stuck on the specifics. And whatever you do, don't quit.

CHAPTER 6

The Great Pleasure in Life

Have you ever had a conversation with someone and before long you realize that nearly everything that comes out of their mouth has something to do with why you *shouldn't* be doing something? Or they spend thirty minutes grumbling about what you should have done? If you haven't, had that experience, then guess what? The moment you decide you're going to be self-employed, you will!

People with negative attitudes will come crawling out of the woodwork. Most of these negative people will fall into one or more of the categories concerning minding your associations, described in Chapter Three. People like these don't intend to be negative, but will give you every reason under the sun why doing whatever you're doing won't work or can't be done a certain way. My advice?

Do it anyway!

Some time ago, I started a cleaning business out of my garage. My son had just been born and was only a few months old. Although my little cleaning business was coming along nicely, things were tight financially and we needed cash. Looking at the skills and resources that I had available, it occurred to me that about a year ago I had heard some information about a possible work source. That "work" consisted of high-rise window cleaning.

I'd only seen high-rise window cleaning being done once. I also knew that not many people jumped at the chance to work several stories in the air. Doing one of these window jobs would bring me much-needed cash, so I set out to find one. After roughly two weeks of soliciting, I landed and scheduled my first high-rise.

Problem was, high-rise window cleaning required special tools and I had no equipment. In short order I went to a supply company to get the equipment I needed. That's when the supply company told me that some of what I needed would have to be ordered.

After consulting my calendar, it appeared that my equipment would arrive exactly a week before I would start the job. So I placed the order. Now I just had to figure out how to pay for the equipment when the order arrived. I had roughly two weeks. I took inventory of skills and resources I had available to me at the time and discovered that I had carpet cleaning equipment and enough solution to clean quite a bit of carpet.

So I set out to get a carpet job. In the process of getting a carpet job, which I did, I also got a small floor job and a small janitorial account – more than enough to pay for the equipment I needed.

I was ready the week of the expected high-rise equipment delivery, but I received no call. When I approached the salesman at the supply company he apologized and said that the equipment was on back order. That meant that it wouldn't arrive until a week after I was supposed to start the high-rise job!

I waited a bit, collected my thoughts, and then called my client. After a brief explanation, not hinting that I'd never done high-rise cleaning before, I requested a job start time for a week later than what we had originally agreed. He accepted. Exactly one week later my equipment arrived. I called the client, arranged roof access, and was sitting on the roof of a twelve-story building, reading the directions on how to put it all together and use it!

The first time I went over the edge of a building was the hardest. You could say after that, it was all down hill. I managed the gear with ease and quickly became accustomed to its use. I finished the job about three days ahead of schedule, got paid and lined up two more high-rise jobs with the same client.

To this day he doesn't know what I went through to do that first job.

I had all sorts of reasons to not go through with what I planned to do. When friends and family asked me what I was doing, and I made the mistake of answering, I got all sorts of reasons to not do the job. There were times during the process when I half-thought they could be right. The reason I succeeded was that I pushed through that fear and did it anyway.

When it comes to fear, I've found people are often strange. They'll say, "No Fear!" and pat themselves on the back but they don't practice it. All the masses do is fear. Which is why in the quest for creating money, few make it.

Fear is the number one reason most people don't as much as grace the door of self-employment.

Fear grows like a snowball. First, people develop lists in their heads as to what they need, why they need it and how they're going to get it. Like a snow ball, the list keeps getting bigger and one by one, fear of overcoming the obstacles gets bigger too.

Then people make the mistake of voicing that fear to their friends and family. Since friends and family have their own fears that they're struggling to overcome, fear multiplies.

Eventually, worries of the past, present and future

become moot because nothing happens. People quit. They don't even *dare* to do what they or other people say that they should not do! At this point, they mentally lock up, shut down and resign to stick to doing what they currently know what they have been doing. As a result, any progress in their finances that may have been achieved is lost. There is no hope of creating money with this mind set – none.

> *Fear is the number one reason people don't so much as grace the door of self-employment.*

Please understand and accept that the stars will not always fall into perfect alignment with everything that you choose to do. You may not have all the tools or equipment needed to do your job. You may not have all the capital required for you to complete a certain task. You may not drive the right car or wear the right clothes or speak properly, etc.

Do it anyway!

Move forward anyway! Don't let people, places or circumstances stop you or prevent you from pushing and driving towards your goal. Be mindful of the future but concern yourself with what is happening right now at this present moment – today!

Fear can and often does manage to sabotage your motivation for creating money. In the chapters you've read so far, which of the ideas are impossible to begin? Notice that I'm not asking which are impossible to accomplish *now*. You won't be able to do everything today. But if you don't conquer fear, you won't accomplish anything. Leave fear behind. Do what can be done *today*.

Today, by reviewing the skills and resources that are available to you, can you make a list of possible businesses you could start? Can you make a list of various business contacts that could help you in the venture you've chosen? Can you start a search for your counsel? Can you define the people in your life who produce negativity and establish ways and methods to avoid them? Can you create a "need to read" book list and start working towards developing your reading habit? Can you make this book list even though you don't own some of the titles on the list?

Get it?

Make plans. Prepare to the best of your ability but don't let the "don't haves" and the "needs" stop you from moving toward your goals. Don't do it. Maybe like me, you discover that the "need" of the right equipment to actually do the job isn't as important as actually *getting* the job. So get the job and work out the details later.

Keep it simple. There is no need to complicate things. Complicating things is what every one does. Train your mind to see things as simply as possible.

Reduce every situation, circumstance or problem to its lowest common denominator. Then address it at that level – simple. With practice, you'll find that "lowest common denominator" reasoning goes beyond business, self-employment or creating money. In time, this type of simplified thinking will spill over into all the areas of your life.

By simplifying, you'll actually be freeing your mind from all the "stuff" that people, friends, family, co-workers, etc. unconsciously impose on you every day. All the so called "rules" and "guidelines" in the ways of going about our daily lives, although may prove necessary in "living," become stifling when attempting to tap into the creativity required for creating money. So if someone tells you something can't be done – challenge it.

Ask why and then analyze the explanation. Seek out reasons and ways to make it work, don't just accept what appears to be for what actually is.

By doing this, struggles become challenges. Challenges become learning experiences. Learning experiences become small prices to pay for an education. Education has value that equates to dollars, and dollars bring you one step closer to creating money! Every challenge you face in regard to creating money, regardless of how trivial, can be used as a feather in your cap assisting you in your ultimate goal.

When you recognize that, your days of running from challenges will stop. You begin to welcome them. You walk through each day, each circumstance, and each challenge with the knowledge that you can't be beat. That you *can* win! From that point on when you encounter problems, circumstances, or struggles that make people around you cringe in fear, you will stand tall, unafraid, and confident in your acquired ability to overcome them.

There is a saying—I'm not sure who said it—that states: "The Great Pleasure in Life is doing what people say you cannot do". It's true. Nothing gives me more pleasure than succeeding when someone has told me I'll fail.

Nothing makes me smile more than when someone looks at what I'm doing or what I've said and responds with, "You're crazy." I smile because I know that at that very moment, my actions, my words, and what I'm doing pulls that person out of his comfort zone and stretches his mind. I am showing them, at that very moment, what I have become accustomed to. The thought processes of thinking "outside of the box" that I have adopted have opened up the door to countless ways of creating money. Regardless of the size of the cheering section on your side, push towards the goal and leave the questions and wonderings to the people sitting on the sidelines.

CHAPTER 7

Tarbosh

Nearly everything that relates to acquiring money stems from a person's self-esteem. Every project, every building built, every product produced and sold has been done so through the inherent belief in the person who created it and belief in his ability. Every one. Belief in one's self, in one's capabilities is essential, a requirement of anyone who wishes to create money.

In 1996 I was working as an insurance agent for the Mutual Of Omaha Insurance Company. The sales I was generating at the start of that year were slow, very slow and with each month that passed my finances were becoming increasingly more difficult to manage. Drumming up "leads" required a ton of phone work and "cold calls" were pretty much a given.

Every Monday night we had what we called a Monday

night phone clinic. Each Monday evening for two hours all of us agents would meet at the office and spend two long grueling hours making call after call, trying to set an appointment for the week. The target closing ratio was for approximately every 100 contacts (meaning you actually spoke to someone) you would set ten appointments. Out of those ten appointments set and run, two would buy and out of those two only one would actually pass the underwriter. In order to pay my expenses and survive financially, I needed to sell at least eight to ten policies a month. At the beginning of that year, I wasn't doing that.

Bills were stacking up. But far worse, my attitude and emotions showed in everything I did. If I landed an appointment, my eagerness in closing would kill the deal and the prospect wouldn't write with me. If I was able to get a client to write a policy with me, it wouldn't pass underwriting. I was crashing hard. Feeling like a failure was a clear and ever present reality I felt every day when I walked in the door of my home. At one point, things got so bad, I stopped coming home.

Then one Monday night, after a long night of making calls, I realized things had become pretty quiet. All of the other agents had already gone home for the evening. All except one.

I was feeling pretty beat-up as I meandered through

the cubicles. I was surprised to find a guy named Tom, still sitting at his desk, working the phone. Tom was a veteran agent. He had been working as an agent for over ten years and during that time had made a lot of money, so seeing him working the phones so fervently made me question why he was still at the office.

When he hung up his phone I asked, "What's up?"

He asked me what I meant.

I said, "Well, I'm just wondering why you're working so late?"

He said, "'Cause I'm on *fire*, dude!" That response was not what I expected to hear.

I gave him a questioning look.

He asked me how I'd been doing.

I told him that things had been tough. I'd been getting the piss kicked out of me. I probably wouldn't be going home that night. I'd hang out at the office and crash in my chair.

He just looked at me and smiled. His reaction kind of miffed me. What kind of guy was amused by my feelings of misery?

I asked him why he was smiling.

He said, "You need Tarbosh!"

I must have looked confused. "Tarbosh? What's that?"

He smiled again. "Not what," he explained. "Who."

He told me that Tarbosh was someone who worked for him occasionally. He'd be willing to introduce me to him.

Immediately upon hearing of this "Tarbosh," my mood improved. I thought, *Wow! This is a veteran agent who's willing to let me use one of his best appointment setters to drum up some much needed appointments!* I got a little excited and I said, "Great! Can I hire him? Would he be willing to work for me?"

Tom chuckled and said, "Sure!"

I said, "Great! When can I meet him?"

With that, Tom scooted to the edge of his chair, looked me in the eye and said, "Now repeat after me . . ." He changed the tone of his voice a bit as he said, "Hello, My name is Tarbosh and I work for Jacob at Mutual of Omaha!"

I stepped back and said, "What?" Why was Tom messing with me?

He began laughing profusely at my bewildered expression, knowing that he had stretched my mind well beyond its reasonable limits. I got a little angry and told him to stop messing with me, that I was in real trouble here and that I needed help, not some fictitious mind game. He stopped laughing.

Then he said, "I'm not messing with you. Tarbosh is as real as you make him. Unlike you, Tarbosh drives the nicest cars, lives in the nicest homes, and eats the finest foods. All of his bills are paid. He takes vacations every month to exotic places." He smiled a bit. "And his girl never has a headache."

It took me a moment to process what he was saying. Then I said, "Yeah, but *you're* Tarbosh!"

He shook his head. "No, I'm not. Not yet." He leaned closer. "But sometimes I call on him, my alter ego that I have created, to give me the focus I need for what I need to accomplish." He smiled again. You see, unlike me, Tarbosh has everything. He needs nothing and because of that his mind is at peace, serene and focused. He's a master salesman!

"So, when things get tough, when I'm feeling the weight of the phone and it feels so heavy that I can hardly pick it up, I utilize the feeling of being Tarbosh to lift it."

I was dumbfounded. I said, "*That's* how you're setting all of these appointments?!"

His response was a simple yes.

I talked to him a bit more about the details of creating my own version of "Tarbosh." I learned that in truth, "Tarbosh" can be whomever or whatever you make it. It's that simple.

You're not trying to trick yourself or become something you can't be. You're not trying to become a phony. If you use your own version of Tarbosh when problems, circumstances and situations that cause you grief arise in your life, you'll rise above them mentally.

As you imagine your life without these problems, you will truly become "Tarbosh." By *acting* confident, focused and serene, you will *become* confident, focused and serene. Your outlook will *actually change*. As a result, your situation or circumstance will change too.

Adopt an attitude of success in everything you do, every circumstance, every situation, every curve ball you're thrown.

For the rest of the year, I practiced doing business with Tarbosh at my side. As a result, I ran more appointments than any other agent in that office and I sold more life insurance than any other Mutual agent in the State of Oregon that year. I even have a little plastic trophy to prove it. Tarbosh was in me all along, but I had to believe and allow Tarbosh to shine. I was successful because Tom was willing to show me the Tarbosh in me.

Your opinion of yourself is very important in regard to the level of your success. One thing that can definitely be said about people who have amassed great wealth is that they have overcome themselves. They have faced their greatest fears within and have over come them.

In time and with practice, you won't need to utilize the services of Tarbosh. In time, who he is and what he represents will become a part of you. When encountering various rejections or delays you will simply smile and maintain your focus because you will see the long term result and in your mind you'll already be there. When Tarbosh is on your side, you'll see more clearly.

With your vision unclouded, you'll be able to carry out each task, confident of its successful outcome in the long term.

By adopting a feeling of confidence in everything you do, people will likely challenge you. Many people may mistake confidence for ego. But there's a huge difference.

Puffed-up people with too much ego are often defensive, self-centered and afraid. This type of self-centered ego rears its ugly head when people have failed and are filled with fear at the thought of failing again. They often adopt an attitude of can't, won't or the worst attitude of all: giving up or becoming apathetic.

In contrast, a person's true confidence is evident *regardless* of fear. The confident person succeeds by demonstrating proven results. Once you begin to see *yourself* as Tarbosh—the confident, focused, peaceful part of you—you'll begin to recognize that it is Tarbosh's attitude that's the missing link to every thing that is needed to be successful.

Notice I didn't say that a confident person always expects instant results. Many times, people aren't successful because they aren't willing to see things in the long term. If results are less than hoped for, these people give up or even worse, tell themselves they can't do much of anything. These people are missing the valuable lesson of rejection. Rejection, or getting a "no" answer, should be an important part of your success strategy.

Embrace rejection. Rejection is your friend. Rejection doesn't mean, "No." Rejection means, "Not now," "I'm not ready," or "I need more information." In many cases, rejection means, "Try harder!" Understanding this is critical. With every rejection you're given, you will come to know and understand the process—and be that much closer to your goal.

Whatever you're seeking, understanding what rejection truly means will come to you through *persistence*. With persistence, you will never again allow your mind to issue you a defeat.

Persistence is important. Because of it, you'll know nothing is over until you allow it to be over – until you quit. So don't quit. Adopt an attitude of success in everything you do, every circumstance, every situation, every curve ball you're thrown. When things don't go as you want them to, collect your thoughts, remember what rejection is, smile and push forward.

Persistence will help you develop confidence. You will develop confidence because you know what you're capable of. You know who you are and what you can do. You know what challenges you have faced and what you have overcome. So approach each new challenge in confidence that it will be overcome! Adopt the Tarbosh kind of confidence, embrace it, and practice it. You will become the "missing link" in whatever equation you are trying to solve.

Say to yourself, "Regardless of the circumstance or situation, I *know* that I am the missing link." Whatever it is that I may do, when I put my mind to it, I will be the best. If it's a business that is struggling or failing I *know* it's because I'm not present in it. When I walk into a room, I own it. If it's a sunny day – it's sunny for me. Arguments stop when I show up.

Rejection has become my friend, my greatest ally. I welcome its arrival because it whispers to me. Rejection reminds me of who I am—whatever the situation, I can handle it. I can't be beat. I will not lose. I will persist and I WILL WIN!

Practice these affirming thoughts until you make them your own. Practice until you can feel them in your gut. You *are* the missing link needed in every situation – YOU.

The very presence of YOU demands success. You're unlike anything anyone has ever seen before. You are unique, the one thing needed, required for anything to be great. Free the "Tarbosh" in you, see yourself for who you really are. Own it.

CHAPTER 8

Cash is King

Like many things in life, acquiring and maintaining money is contingent on your perception of it. Friends, co-workers, and family may have strong opinions about how and where you should be using or spending your money. These perceptions of money may influence you; they may have even been your own perceptions at one time.

I'm going to tell you another secret to creating and maintaining money. Regardless of the information you receive from various outside influences surrounding you, remember one thing – Cash is King.

Money in hand equals opportunity. The more money you have in hand at any given moment, the more you'll be able to spot and take advantage of a financial opportunity when it arises. Because of that, you need to always be striving for liquidity.

"Liquidity" refers to money that is readily available to you whenever you need it. The practice of liquidity is relatively simple. Do nothing, purchase nothing, engage in nothing without keeping liquidity in mind. Maintaining a consistent level of cash on hand, not only allows you to take full advantage of money-making opportunities that arise. Positive cash flow also frees up your mind to be fully focused on the task at hand. Being focused equates to more expendable time. In order to do that you need to fully understand the difference between "Credit" and "Leveraging."

Credit, in the way that most people choose to use it, robs people of their expendable time.

With each new purchase, each new monthly expense added, another hour of your time is sold. Each hour of your time that is sold depletes your available expendable time. Ultimately, you bind yourself indefinitely to whatever money-making vehicle you're driving.

If you acquire and use credit that you cannot immediately repay at any given moment, you're in a situation of unrest with no peace. Using credit in this way is essentially the selling of your time, your options, your opportunities, and the very essence of your soul. Credit is what the masses use.

Credit, used in this manner, is for "broke" people. These people can't afford to pay the total sum for something they want or need, so they agree to make small payments, plus whatever interest rate the credit company charges. A modestly priced item could end up costing much more than the retail price.

In contrast, people who create money use "leveraging." At first glance, leveraging appears very similar to credit. In both cases, you take out a loan or make a purchase "on time," by making payments. The difference between credit and leveraging is that those who leverage don't really need the loan or note to make the purchase. They are in a sense, increasing their expendable dollars to increase their opportunity potential.

To simplify the concept, let me explain it like this: In order to leverage your money, if you had one hundred dollars, you wouldn't spend your one hundred dollars to make a purchase. You'd make the desired purchase via a loan or note. That way you'd have the value of the item purchased *and* you'd still have your original one hundred dollars.

Next, you'd take the one hundred dollars that you still had and put it in savings or in an interest bearing account *for the life of the loan.*

In this way, your money has remained liquid and your time has too. At any given moment you have the ability to pay the loan off in full. People who create money do not engage in credit. They utilize the power of leveraging, which keeps their minds free and allows them to take advantage of money-making opportunities when they arise.

Sounds great doesn't it? Sure, unless you're like most people, who have used credit and are now in debt. But there is a way out. You can begin to practice liquidity right now. Start by changing the way you *think* about what you want and what you need. From now on, in your mind, Cash is King. Obtaining and retaining cash is now your number one priority.

From now on, credit is now something you choose to avoid at all costs. When you're cash poor, credit's only use—and only if required in order to operate—is in acquiring major purchases such as a car or a home. Pay for everything else in cash or else don't purchase it.

Stop now and think about what you truly *need*. Not what you want, but what you need. What do you absolutely have to have in order to live? What is required? Food? A place to live? Transportation? Clothing? What else?

Make a list of your absolute necessities and assign a dollar amount to them. Then look for ways to reduce your expenses. Cut, cut, cut out as many expenses as you can. Your goal is to free up expendable dollars and free up the time needed to earn those dollars so you can be focused on creating money.

Cut, cut, cut out as many expenses as you can. Your goal is to free up expendable dollars and free up the time needed to earn those dollars so you can be focused on creating money.

When you're finished, you'll typically have a number that is much less than what you're used to paying. This amount will become your break-even number. This figure is the *minimum amount of money* you will need to produce every month in order to operate.

Next, make a list of all your debt. These are any expenses that you don't absolutely *have to have* in order to operate. Ask yourself, "If this was paid off today, would I miss it?" If the answer is *no*, it goes on your debt list.

Hang on—this is where the fun starts.

You're now going to be incredibly creative when it comes to paying your debt, keeping in mind that your goal is to free up your cash and your time. The most important thing to remember at this point is no new debt. That's right. If you hope to create a debt-free liquid cash flow, you must be willing to keep from incurring any new debt. You probably already have debts that need to be wiped out.

First thing you're going to do is to look at your existing debt list. Put them in order from highest to lowest. Then add up all the money you're currently using to pay toward the debt on that list.

Next, for every payment you're currently paying, cut that payment in half. That's right, reduce your payment by fifty percent. Now, allocate that new lower number as the new payment for that debt. For now, forget about your credit score! Remember, you've already decided that credit is only to be used for major purchases such as a home or a car. Right now you're not going to be doing either, so worrying about your credit score does you no good.

Keep in mind that *always* cash trumps credit. Until you're in a position to leverage, don't worry about your credit.

Write letters to all your creditors, stating your situation and what you're trying to do. Keep a contact list for each person you talk to for each debt. Jot down that person's name, title, department and the date. Try to work only with that person until the debt is paid. If you can, ask for that worker by name, or get their direct line phone number.

Take the other half of the money you have cut from your debt and add it up. Whatever that amount comes up to, you're going to now apply it all toward the *lowest bill* on your debt list. In some cases the amount will pay that bill off in its entirety, in others it may take a few months.

Once that bill is paid off, take the payment you would have normally paid to it and apply it to the next lowest bill on your debt list. Repeat this process until all of your debts on your list are paid in full.

At this point, you will have more expendable cash on hand. Less of your time will be required to cover basic monthly expenses. During this process you are going to consistently be looking for ways to reduce expenses, increase your revenue and *avoid any new debt.*

As you look for ways to avoid new debt, you may need to evaluate how you normally purchase different items. For instance, if you are sincere about lowering your operating expenses don't rely on credit to clothing. Instead, utilize discount or second hand stores. Food is another area where using credit doesn't help you in your goal of creating money. Learn to shop for grocery items that are large enough for left-overs or used for more than one kind of meal. Limit restaurant meals as much as possible, brown-bagging lunches and preparing meals that can be frozen and reheated. Monitor lighting and heating expenses for reasons other than just helping the environment.

Other cost-cutting ideas include carrying the minimum requirements on insurance policies or increasing deductibles to reduce premiums. Remember, the goal is to reduce expenses and increase expendable revenue in preparation for creating money.

Auto purchases should be looked at differently too. Automobiles are little more than tools that you use to get from point "A" to point "B." With that in mind, the only requirements are that they have four decent tires; that the car starts when you turn the key and that the car runs at a reasonably efficient level. Auto payments are an "expendable cash" killer and should be avoided. Buy used and pay in cash when ever possible. If making payments are required, buy used, put as much cash down as you can and pay off as soon as possible.

You can do this by focusing on reducing the sticker price at the time of the purchase. Don't let the salesman turn your focus on the monthly payment. By keeping your focus on negotiating a reduced sticker price of the automobile at the time of the purchase you will be reducing the monthly payment. Set the terms for the maximum months available to keep the payment low with the intent of paying it off early.

Avoid adding to your loan any extended warranties, services or additions. If you're concerned about the automobile breaking down, fix it yourself or find a good mechanic that you trust but don't include that stuff in your loan. These add-ons will increase your monthly payment and you'll end up paying nearly double the interest!

Looking for low cost housing is important too. Remember, we're looking to free up dollars and expendable time. Check into housing that covers the necessities. Again, take into consideration what you can't live without.

Plan to buy your dream home *after* you've become financially sound. If you can't pay cash for it or put down a large down payment don't buy it. If you do you'll simply have a slightly different landlord *and* you'll have sold your time and expendable cash to get it. Unless it's paid for, you don't truly own it. So don't be in a hurry to get it until you can own it.

Why would I say that? Common knowledge says that buying a home—the American Dream—is better than renting. But let's run the numbers. If you rent a home and invest the difference over a thirty year period (the standard length of a fixed mortgage) rather than buying a home and making payments over a thirty year period, renting and investing out performs the equity generated over the course of that thirty years nearly every time! And it will be liquid – meaning you will actually be able to use it whenever you need it. Access to those funds will not be contingent on the sale of your house.

The key in all of this is the investment part, which is one reason why most people don't do it. In order for this scenario to work properly, people who rent must invest the difference that they save from not purchasing.

It takes discipline to invest consistently. It requires much less thought to simply make a mortgage payment. If you currently own a home or are making payments on a home that has any equity in it at all – sell it. Use it to pay off what debt you have and invest it in something that actually makes you money. Use it to free up your time and resources, allowing your mind to be clear so that you can focus on new creative ways of creating money.

Quit spending your time, effort and energy working towards the accumulation of "things" that ultimately *cost* you money and pursue the development of ways to *make* you money. Cover your basic living expenses. Automobiles are simply tools. Houses are just big boxes, that vary in shapes and sizes, in which we need to live.

Keep the thought of creating money in mind at all times while going about your daily activities. Think about it. How do you expect to tap into the creativity of creating money that you are capable of producing, while constantly being bombarded with your need of financial survival? You may have a ton of ideas and ways of making money inside you, none of which are accessible to you because your expendable time is already used up. Your expendable resources are already sold. Free them up! Consistently look for ways to reduce costs and increase revenue. Actively pursue the increase of your expendable time and money. Never forget – Cash is King.

CHAPTER 9

Swimming with Sharks

Early on in my quest for creating money, I had the opportunity of meeting a young man that who much farther along in the process than I was. At the time I was roughly twenty-four years old and he was about twenty-six. At the age of twenty-six, this young man owned two restaurants and a cleaning business. This was someone I could learn something from and I knew it. I asked to meet with him for a chance at employment.

We set up a time to meet at one of his restaurants, I dressed in a suit and was a few minutes early. After I was seated he stopped by the table briefly to tell me he would be a few minutes late but that he would be there shortly. So I waited. Time seemed to drag by and occasionally he would walk by my table, smile and tell me just a few more minutes. My response, of course, was always a no problem, sounds great. We carried on like that for nearly two hours. Always polite, very cordial, but I wasn't leaving and he knew it.

Finally he sat down at the table, apologized for his delay and asked me about myself and what I wanted. I told him that I was an insurance agent doing sales for the Mutual of Omaha Company and that I wanted him to hire me for a janitorial position in his cleaning company. He seemed just as baffled at the request as some of my co-workers did at my office. He chose instead to hire me as a sales rep. for his cleaning company. We negotiated a rate of pay and I began the following Monday. In a very short time I was operating and managing his cleaning business for him. About a year and a half later I bought it from him.

This guy was very aggressive in his business approach and we had become good friends. After he sold his cleaning business to me, he set out to open a club next door to one of his restaurants. When it opened, he was literally swimming in cash. Sitting at the bar one morning, him and I were literally counting stacks of $20, $50 and $100 bills totaling well over $20,000.00 that had been collected at the door for *one* night. That didn't include the money that was generated from the food, lotto or bar sales. I had never seen so much money in my life. The sheer volume of money that he had generated in one night was enough to make my head spin.

All was not well in paradise, though. He had created volume in his cash flow for sure but his debt load was incredibly large too. Over the course of a few months, managing that debt became increasingly difficult.

By building the club he'd maxed out his leveraging capabilities. He was operating on credit. When the lending institutions refused to offer any more credit, his only option was to turn to cash on hand in order to get the club ready for opening. Doing this depleted his expendable resources and even though the club finally opened and was doing well it was not enough to keep up with the snowball of debt that the building of it had created.

Liens had been filed, judgments followed and garnishments proved to be a very difficult thing to manage.

Although I hadn't been working for him at the time, he remained my friend and I offered to do what I could to help him. I'll never forget sitting with him at his attorney's office listening to his attorney talk about the latest lien that had been filed. It was a place I never thought he would be. We had wracked our brains trying to manage it. We were extremely creative in our approach to fixing it. Ultimately his attorney's advice was simple: "Tender the money." I can still see the expression on his face and the sound of his voice when he said it. It felt as if a huge hammer just fell. We had no other options, it was all we could do and if we couldn't do that – it was over.

The months that followed were grueling and they ended in court with my friend relinquishing the keys to his businesses. He lost them all. With some minor help from me, he's back in the cleaning business and on his way to rebuilding. The lessons and experience we both gained, having gone through it, have proven to be life changing.

When working towards creating money there are a few things you need to remember. You're essentially swimming in a very vast sea of other people and other businesses all trying to build and grow. They are not always there to help or assist you. They are in a sense – sharks.

They will wait for you to make a mistake, look for signs of bleeding and then strike. You need to always be mindful of that and make sure to protect yourself. Always monitor your debt load and don't overextend your self. Being aggressive in business is great but not if it costs you what you have created.

Keeping cash flow moving is important but not as important as what cash you have made available to you on hand. Negotiating your terms on your debt is great but make sure to pay them. If not you'll be facing legal challenges just like my friend.

Taxes are another area of concern. Speaking from personal experience, I can honestly say in no uncertain terms: DO NOT GET BEHIND ON YOUR TAXES! The government is very unforgiving. It doesn't matter how or why you're behind, they get their money first and they'll file a UCC (Uniform Commercial Code) filing to ensure of it. Establish specific contacts if you can and work to maintain any arrangements. Ultimately, with these sharks, you *will* "tender the money" or they'll just take it.

Managing and maneuvering yourself in the sea of business, although challenging at times, is very rewarding, but you must stick to the basics. The basics being, keep your debt load low, watch your cash flow and maintain an adequate level of cash on hand at all times. It's not just important to do that to take advantage of opportunities and to maintain peace of mind. It's also important to do this so you can protect what you've created.

When establishing business contacts and relationships, remember the people you're working with are in business too and not all of them are honest. Not all of them are going to be working in your best interest. CPAs, bookkeepers, attorneys, contractors, insurance companies, lending institutions, supply companies, etc. all have their own wants and needs to think about and be mindful of. Watch them, closely.

By not doing so you're setting yourself up for theft. Many of these people will steal from you by way of extra billings, interest, penalties, extra fees, overcharges, etc. If and when you don't pay, they'll turn on you fast and go for blood through liens, judgments and garnishments. Regardless of who they are as people, when it comes to business, they are *not* your friends.

That attitude seems a little hard core doesn't it? Listen, once again, I'm not saying these are necessarily bad people. But the decision to work with you on a debt or offer help by way of more time is often not up to just them.

They answer to other people, other people within their organizations who may not have been invited to the barbeque at your home. So, making friends with your business contacts is great and it will assist you in business but it only goes so far when the rubber meets the road and you're up against it.

The key is to never put yourself or them into that position. You can avoid these problems by being responsible enough to watch your debt load and maintain a certain level of cash on hand. It can be difficult to remember this for sure, especially when you're on a growth spike, but it's the one thing that will keep you sound when rough weather comes—and it will come—so prepare for it.

Every living person that has a household to take care of and manage is, in a sense, in business. Sure, they may just be working at a job but if you look at their situation from a business perspective, they are essentially operating a small business out of their home.

This home business comes complete with a source of revenue that is generated, in most cases via a job. The home business has overhead, by way of monthly living expenses. Some of these expenses are "fixed," some are "variable." Home businesses have "supply" costs such as food and gas, a client such as their place of work, and employees such as kids, family members etc. The home business residence is the business address, it's required to carry insurance and if the home business owners are married, their marriage certificate is their business license.

The point here is, you run a business whether you call it that or not. And although the sharks circling a home business may differ from those of a conventional business, they're still sharks. Worse still, these sharks are often friends or loved ones. Keep your eye out for those (even your closest relationships) who might smell blood in the water. By that, I mean, a friend or relative who sees you prospering may decide to demand a piece of the success you've worked hard to build. So, the need to be mindful of the sharks in the pool you're swimming in is still of great importance.

With that in mind, who's your auto insurance through? Or your life insurance through? Your health insurance?

Who files your taxes? Where do you bank? Who handles your investments? Who wrote your car loan?

Are they a friend of yours, maybe a family member? Have you maintained a business relationship with them or have you made it personal?

By that I mean, are you getting the best rate or are you paying more for the coverage and services you need because they are a friend or relative? Ask yourself these questions, because if saving you money or reducing your costs is something you're not willing to do for sake of maintaining a relationship, you need to re-evaluate that relationship.

When things are good and you're paying "on time" every thing works fine and friends and family assisting you in your needs is great. But when things get tight and you're under the gun to perform, are you doing yourself or them any favors when you put them between your financial well-being and the people they answer to? Not in my opinion.

Consider who you have and what you have them doing. Don't put friends and family members in positions that may make them behave like a shark. Because make no mistake, if you're slowly bleeding financially, the companies they work for will eat you.

Swimming with sharks isn't a cause for concern or a reason to not do something. Their presence has always been there in what you do. The key to swimming with sharks is to recognize it for what it is and don't allow yourself to fall prey to sharks. Keep your debt load low, build your cash reserves and don't over extend yourself. Only then can you move forward in your quest for creating money unencumbered by the cold hard reality of the sharks around you.

> *The key to swimming with sharks is to recognize it for what it is and don't allow yourself to fall prey to sharks. Keep your debt load low, build your cash reserves and don't over extend yourself.*

Chapter 10
Let it go

When you picked up this book I bet I could tell you what was on your mind – money. My hope is that during your reading of this book, you have been able to examine what you know of money and increase your knowledge of how it really works. But you need to keep in mind why you truly want and need it.

Your quest for creating money isn't simply about *acquiring* money. That's something people don't always understand. Money isn't what you seek. What you truly want is what it *provides*. Money can provide the lifestyle you want to live and the expendable time you need to spend doing what you want to do. But money itself is sort of cold. Remember Scrooge McDuck, who was such a miser that he could only count his money? He wasn't willing to let a cent of it go. Don't be like McDuck, so consumed in your pursuit of money for what you want that you fail to recognize what you already have.

If you've done everything I've recommended in this book, then you're ready for what could be the most important lesson: Let it go.

Life is about living. You have to make sure you're still living it. I hope this book has helped you recognize your need of money, educate yourself on its proper use, mind your associations, practice the laws of giving and receiving, think outside of the box, maintain a positive self image, and remember cash is king while staying on the lookout for "sharks." With commitment, practice and persistence, you're going to teach yourself to do all these things, so you can truly live in the way that you desire. Don't allow yourself to get so caught up in your thoughts or actions of creating money that you forget this fundamental truth: Don't work to create money for its own sake. You must be willing to let money help you live.

Besides, as Scrooge McDuck learned, money can't give anyone what it's incapable of providing. Friends and family members who may not be the best candidates to associate with in regard to money can still be a vital part of your life in other ways. These relationships might help you maintain a positive self-image, and they may even observe and learn a thing or two from you. In the meantime, let it go.

Don't make the mistake of placing more value on acquiring money than recognizing what is truly important in life. Keep your quest for creating money in perspective. Money is a tool. That's all it is, and it should be treated as such.

Don't allow your quest for money to divide you from family members or rob you of relationships – let it go.

In the end, your reasons for acquiring and needing money are to enhance the things you value, not to lose or destroy them over money. You seek what it brings. Ultimately, you want to be in a position to expand and do more with what you've acquired, setting in motion the laws of giving and receiving. You want to become the rock that the people around you look up to and rely on.

Becoming a rock, or a person others look up to, is about more than how much money you can amass. You can probably name people whose wealth is overshadowed by their shark-like business practices. Creating money on the backs of others generates fear, not trust. Building character while you create money for yourself is the only path to true financial success.

As you put these common sense ideas about money into practice, give back in ways that involve more than just money. Be honorable in your dealings and just in your rebuke and you will become known as a person of true character. Reach out to that person who chooses you to be counsel. Show that person the books to read, the positive attitude to model, and the way to get out of debt. Qualities such as these can't be purchased, but they can be practiced. In your pursuit of money, you must either encourage these inherent qualities to grow or they may be stolen from you through deceit.

You may be told that in order to succeed, a businessperson must behave in cutthroat or even dishonest ways. It's not true. Standard business practice may tell you, encourage you to behave like a shark, preying on other weaker businesses. You don't have to. In fact, I believe you are more likely to succeed if you don't—and you'll be able to sleep better at night, too.

You know right from wrong. Success, as I define it, doesn't require you act in ways that go against your values or your conscience. If everyone is against your doing something you know to be right - do it anyway. If everyone is urging you to do something you know to be wrong – don't do it, no matter who says it's OK.

Think outside the "box," remember? Cut your own path. Do it your own way.

Don't allow the fears of "broke" people influence or deter you. Regardless of the economy, gas prices, tax increases, etc. Remain focused on your goal.

Remember that all those challenges are nothing more than reasons for you to push and succeed in your quest for creating money. So address each one with the attitude that you will succeed, that you will be like water. Like water, you will go over them, around them or through them, but you'll face them all – with no fear. You must not allow the grumblings of the people around you to stifle your confidence in yourself or in your ability to perform.

You are the missing link in any equation. You were born in success. Nothing that this life sends your way will *ever* change that. There is no one like you and when you leave this earth no one will replace you. You are unique.

Understand the difference between ego and confidence. Ego is trying to impress those around you that you're the greatest. Ego is often bragging without substance—as lot of hot air about nothing. The essence of confidence is the belief in yourself and your ability. Confidence quietly goes about getting things done without much fanfare. Ego comes from fear. Confidence comes from belief and trust.

Be confident in your abilities – always. If the entire world is against you, and at times it may feel that way, you need to remember to be on your own side. When faced with problems, struggles, circumstances that you need to overcome, remember to think of obstacles for what they are – temporary.

Nothing you're currently facing will be a concern to

you, like it is at this moment, ten years from now - find comfort in that.

Keep your focus on the goal. Don't allow the challenges you face to change you into someone you're not. Don't allow your own mind to trick you into thinking you're something you're not. Remain true to yourself and the ones you care about.

Remember to expand your knowledge by reading as widely as possible. Utilize your time spent working to educate yourself, through reading, about the various ways to make money work for you. Then, use the information and resources available to you to do that—make your money work.

If you have an asset, put it to good use by applying it to help you create more expendable time and money. Don't spend your expendable time and money in servitude to maintain your asset. Solidify your revenue source first, and then acquire assets. If you do, you'll free up your mind and expendable time to be able to tap into your source of creativity. Use your creativity to think. Think and establish new methods, new ways of creating money.

Most people start working as teenagers and hope to retire at age sixty-five. Today, it's a fact that most aren't able to retire. If you're destined to spend that time working anyway, why not attempt to discover ways to create money? By practicing these common sense ideas about creating money, you'll have a much better chance of shortening your sentence of working hard to scrape by.

Dare to spend time thinking. Think about the expendable time and resources you currently have available. Look for ways to expand and grow these blocks of time and resources. If a skill or education is needed to do a certain job or run a business, only engage in instruction that helps propel you toward your goal. Don't waste your expendable time and resources to gain approval of someone who is simply offering you a job, unless that job works towards your goal of creating money.

Take a good, long look at your associations. Make adjustments as necessary. Actively pursue establishing a strong counsel. Model strong, honest behavior. By doing so you'll earn the esteem of others and at some point may provide counsel for someone else.

No one arrives at success's door alone– no one. Successful people become successful through the help of the people around them. Regardless of what some may say, when you really look at things, everyone who's successful has had help. Establish a counsel, glean from their wisdom and be open to receive it.

In everything you're doing to create money, remember that time is a poor measure of success. It's never accurate –never! Make sure you spend your time learning, thinking, growing in knowledge. Be tenacious with your goals and never give up.

Establish a positive opinion of money and what it truly is, and what it can and can't do. Discipline yourself to learn about it, study it. Carefully choose your associations. Build a counsel. Seems like a lot of stuff to do and remember, doesn't it?

If you make up your mind, all these components of success will become a habit. Habits form after you've done something for at least thirty days, so stay focused. After a month or so, the ideas in this book will just become something you do. When you practice teaching yourself to solve problems and reduce costs, you'll find yourself looking to do so in all situations. By being cautious in your business dealings, you'll prevent and reduce your encounters with sharks. You'll learn new skills and establish more confidence to overcome challenges.

Don't watch the clock—this type of success can't be measured in terms of an hourly rate. This isn't a race; it's a marathon. Don't allow a person you associate with or a challenging circumstance to discourage you or deceive you into acting in ways that you know are wrong. You're building character.

Be persistent in your quest for creating money. Actively pursue it to the best of your ability and remember to enjoy this life. Let it go.

Do you know what I mean when I say to "Let it go?" First, understand where you are in the process. Remember when we talked about giving and receiving a few chapters back? Planting "seeds" goes beyond merely giving and receiving. It is, in essence, the start or beginning of anything in regard to creating money. Thoughts, ideas, aspirations all come from a "planting" of "seeds." And with every seed planted, the proper management and maintenance of the seed will produce fruit in its required time. Notice I said "required" time? There is a time element in every seed that is planted. The seed isn't going to bear fruit until the time is right. No amount of interference will speed up the process.

Sometimes remembering this seed and time idea is what helped me be at ease with where I was at and what I was doing financially. It came from the understanding of the natural order of things and how things come to develop. All paths to success begin with seeds. When seeds are planted, managed, maintained and allowed to grow and develop, they will inevitably bear fruit. Until then the best advice is to let it go.

Getting frustrated or impatient over the timing of the fruit makes no sense and serves no purpose if you haven't planted or tended to the seed. Make sense? Think about and understand where you are in your financial endeavors. Do you have a seed? Have you planted it? Are you tending to it?

Are you allowing it the time it takes to grow? If you are, then letting go of when things are going to happen should be easier. Cultivate a clear understanding of the necessary requirements for any task to bear fruit and you will begin to see and understand your place in its process.

Sometimes, for me, the greatest financial growth would come when I simply quit worrying about the timing of the fruit and simply spent my time focusing on tending to my seed. Worrying about the "when" and "how" of the fruit will not help your seeds grow any faster. But worry may jeopardize your ability to tend to your seeds.

So, take note. Tend to your seed and let it go. Be excited with the knowledge that you are headed towards fulfilling a purpose, one that you were born to fulfill, uniquely given to you, unlike anything that has ever been seen before. Apply what you have learned. This is your path. Take it.

About the Author

The concept of Money "Creation" brought to you by someone who has done it.

Through out this book Jacob C. Larson gives you insight into his early perceptions of money, challenges he over came in his personal life and an understanding of his current motivations toward the concept of money "Creation".

Having been raised a "Pastor's Kid", the concept of "creating" money was somewhat foreign and not something that was encouraged for him to pursue. In-spite of having no formal education, no financial background or training what-so-ever, he persisted in studying the subject himself and became self-employed in June of 1996. Since then he has successfully ran a small business for over 15 years, written two books and helped many people improve their financial situation. He is a living testament to the concepts that are outlined in this book and an inspiration to those who would take their first steps toward money "Creation".

Find out more about the Author by going to:

www.buycommonsense.com

www.ingramcontent.com/pod-product-compliance
Lightning Source LLC
Chambersburg PA
CBHW022007170526
45157CB00003B/1179